HOW TO CORRECT THE PROBLEM HORSE

Dave Jones

Bill Weikel, Editor
THE FARNAM HORSE LIBRARY

1

HORSE LIBRARY

The Farnam Horse Library
8701 North 29th Street
Omaha, Nebraska 68112

FRONT COVER
Charlie Carter, trainer for
Bill Nelson's Circle N
Ranch, Paradise Valley,
Arizona, demonstrates
hard-to-load "problem."
Photograph by Theodore
Cogswell, Staff Photographer, Farnam Companies.

**PHOTOGRAPH
ACKNOWLEDGMENTS:**
Dave Jones; Bill Coleman;
The Dave Jones Training
Stable, Tallahassee, Florrida; A. M. Davis, D.V.M.
Photography by Dave
Jones and Bill Coleman.

APRIL 1974
SECOND EDITION

CONTENTS

1 Problem Horses —
    Whence Do They Come?   **4**

2 Some Basic Problems
    And How To Solve Them   **8**

3 Why And How A Horse Is Thrown   **22**

4 Cures For Bad Manners   **27**

5 Bad Experiences
    And Their Remedies   **38**

6 Correcting Performance Faults   **46**

7 On Not Spoiling Horses   **57**

8 Understanding Horses   **60**

9 Conformation Problems   **63**

HOW TO CORRECT THE PROBLEM HORSE

Problems are relative not only to their severity, but also to the *owner-ship* status; what may be a problem horse to one individual might be a dream horse to another. The confirmed bucking horse that no one in the "neighborhood" can ride could be a very dangerous animal to the beginner or intermediate rider, but he could be an extremely valuable asset to a rodeo producer. Similar examples could be cited in almost every class of horse from the Thoroughbred racehorse to the Shetland Pony. It becomes necessary, therefore, to evaluate each horse against his intended use, and to be practical in the decision that must be made regarding whether to spend time, effort and money in his further training, or to trade him for a more suitable mount.

It is also necessary for a great number of horsemen to become more knowledgeable in their abilities to recognize problems. This is very important, not only when the purchase of a horse is involved, but also on a day to day basis as bad habits and small problems begin to take place. Early recognition of *behavior* abnormalties can save weeks, even months, of re-training procedures.

After the ability to recognize problems has been sharpened, and the rider has learned to be more perceptive and sensitive in his daily relationships with his horse, he can then begin to apply his increased knowledge of what to do about problems as they make their appearance. Is it a problem that he can handle himself?

Perhaps one section of this book should have been subtitled "How To Correct The Problem Rider," because many problems with the horse have their origin in some unwitting act or bad habit of the owner or rider. Horses are individuals and even the most experienced trainer sometimes must stand back and carefully re-evaluate the characteristics of a particular animal as they pertain to his training program. There is no one pat answer to everything — to every problem. What may work for one individual, sometimes will not be effective for another. The more knowledgeable one becomes, the more answers he'll have in his "bag of tricks." Awareness, knowledge and experience are three of the most important factors in correcting the problem horse. ■

CHAPTER ONE

PROBLEM HORSES — WHENCE DO THEY COME?

To some degree, all horses are problem horses. There is no such thing as a perfect horse. The horse with only a few minor problems is a jewel. Think of your horse and the things he does wrong, and you'll realize that he is a "problem" horse.

All too often we blame a colt's early handling, his training and the way he's treated rather than laying the blame where it often belongs — on the horse himself. True, thousands of horses are spoiled by poor or stupid trainers. This can't be excused, but we rarely blame the horse himself.

There are good people and bad people. Youngsters from fine homes, with every conceivable advantage, turn bad. Horses too can turn bad as readily as their human counterparts. A wise trainer can generally straighten a bad horse out — by being kind and sensitive, or stern and relentless, as conditions may warrant.

Poor breeding practices have deluged the country with many mediocre and bad dispositioned horses. As more and more people go into the horse business, their possessive pride tells them that they have perfect horses and push the bad product onto more newcomers.

When the American Quarter Horse Association closed its stud book, I wrote a letter of protest. Closing the stud book meant that inspection was no longer necessary. A Quarter Horse stallion would be mated to a Quarter horse mare and the resulting offspring would be a registered Quarter horse — no inspection necessary. I had thought that the inspectors, before the book was closed, were far too lenient in what they passed. Closing the book meant, as far as I could foresee, a degeneration of the Quarter horse.

The inspectors I talked to seemed to think otherwise. One told me that there would be a winnowing out of unfit horses until only the best were commanding enough money to make raising the Quarter horse a practical thing. His thinking was very idealistic. Time has proven me right and him wrong.

My letter to the president of the American Quarter Horse Associaiton was unusual in that it was the only letter received opposing the closing of the stud book. It was read at the annual convention.

No one else protested to the Association, but many breeders I talked to told me that they were opposed, as was I.

I speak of Quarter horses because I am most familiar with them. The story is the same with all breeds except "speed" horses. Horses that have to produce speed must be bred to this end. If possessive pride has much to do with his breeding program, the race horse breeder will soon be out of business.

Poor horses have a start such as this. A man attends a sale. He purchases a colt for $300. He purchases a mare for $200, a filly for $350. He thinks that they're pretty fair horses and that he might make a few dollars on them. The longer he has them, the more he likes them. Pretty soon, in his mind, they're as good as the best. The colt matures into a stallion of breeding age and services the mares and the filly along with a few other mares and fillies he has picked up in the meantime. The resulting offspring can be termed horses — but certainly nothing worth registering. They're not Quarter horses — or Appaloosas — or Arabians; they're just plain horse.

This same man has a friend who wants to start in the horse business. He is easily convinced that buying from his friend is the thing to do. The "breeder" sells his "horses" to the novice, who certainly can't tell a good horse from a bad one and a cycle, like a chain letter, is started. These plugs sell for a lot of money until the people who are at the end of the chain try to sell these horses in a sale or to win something with them at a show. Then they find out what they have. Such happenings have produced thousands of "mongrel" registered horses that can win nothing, do nothing, look terrible, have bad dispositions, and are *really* Problem Horses.

Maybe we should have computers to tell us what a good horse really is. The computer has nothing at stake — no "axe to grind" — has no possessive pride. "Click-clack — whir — buzz — The — horse — you — want — to — buy — is — no — good. — You — must — look — elsewhere — click — clack — buzz."

Guys like me — trainers — who don't have horses for sale — can do better than most at telling a good one from a bad one. We've all ridden good ones and bad ones and have formulated strong opinions about horses. This is my opinion.

It's hard to judge a horse until he's at least two years old. A colt changes. He'll look good at six months of age and then go through a gawky period when he looks terrible. He's pretty well grown up as a two-year old and can then be accurately judged.

To me, conformation is everything. The colt I pick at halter will be the one I'd want to buy and own. He must have a good head and a good way of traveling, besides being built right. This is all included in conformation. The horse with a good head will have a good disposition for he'll have brain room and a large brown mild eye. The only bad horses with good heads have been made that way by their handlers.

We handle many two-year olds that have had no handling until they're of the age to be ridden. I can tell you which ones will be gentle by the width of the forehead and the size and look of the eye. In a horse, the eye is truly the "mirror of the soul." Occasionally I'm fooled by a colt with a bad head who will be gentle and well-mannered. But the "good head" is never naturally mean.

There are stupid people and there are stupid horses. A stupid horse can be a top working horse, but the stupidity presents itself in various forms. We have a mare that is used for wrangling horses. She knows her job and many people have commented on how smart she is. She's not smart, but she does know her job. I can rope a sick or lame mare off her and she'll be perfect. But she can never be tied up for she'd fight until death. She can't learn this one thing. Her offspring have the same trait. This mare is very narrow in the forehead. A better, wider forehead would give her enough room to reason that she must stand when tied. A moron can learn to do a certain job but doing one job well doesn't mean that he has great intelligence.

A reining horse that's a little on the stupid side may continue winning show after show. He may be a consistent winner until he's 20. The more intelligent horse will "scotch" (cheat) his rider and be through after a year or so of competition. Brains aren't always an asset.

The bad headed horse will usually find ways to keep from being ridden. He can learn to sulk, to rear, to rein away or to fret and prance until his rider puts him up to loaf his life away in the barn. When I have a choice, I'll put my saddle on the horse with the good head — good conformation.

It's a fact that a poor trainer can train a horse and come up with passably good results. The horse is very adaptable. Witness how many ways there are to train horses. And the horse generally ends up working in some fashion.

But ignorance and lack of ability have spoiled horses since man first started thinking about getting astride the horse and using him for transportation. There have always been fine horsemen and lousy horsemen. Training has progressed very little over the centuries. We have fine sensitive horsemen and horsewomen. We also have sadists who call themselves trainers. We have the genius and we have the fool.

The "bronc stomper" approaches wary colt. Note hobbles and sideline which will help control horse if he spooks as he is being introduced to saddle.

One doesn't need a diploma to make his living as a trainer. He just says "I'm a trainer and it will cost you X number of dollars to have me work your horses." Many trainers force horses to work — or the horse is afraid not to work. The horses hate and fear man after this guy is done with them. He spoils as many horses as he trains.

One of the hardest things a trainer has to swallow is handing a fine colt, that's working brilliantly, back to his novice owner. The owner knows nothing about riding, much less handling a finely tuned colt. I've had owners spoil a colt in five minutes. The solution to this problem is a tough one. I'm a trainer, not a riding instructor. I do coach the owner as much as I can but I can't turn him into an "instant horseman."

After this "greenhorn" rides his colt for a few months, the colt does nothing well; he is almost totally spoiled. Someone asks, "Who trained that horse?"

"I took him to Dave Jones."

"Oh boy, I'd heard that he couldn't train worth a darn and now I can see it. You should send him back to 'Joe Blow.' He trained my colt and he really works."

That's the way it goes. A trainer's life isn't all sunshine and roses. ■

CHAPTER TWO

SOME BASIC PROBLEMS
AND HOW TO SOLVE THEM

High-Headed

Western riders generally want their horses to work with a low head. The handling horse should work with his neck arched and his chin in. Most Western horses travel with the head down until asked to work. Then many of them will throw his head in the rider's face. We've all been hit in the face by a horse's head.

Conformation has a great deal to do with whether or not a horse will be high-headed. The "ewe-necked" horse — the horse with the neck put on backwards — is always high-headed. The short necked horse has a tendency to throw his head up when worked.

A nice refined neck on the long side, is very desirable. We should think of Arabians and Thoroughbreds when we think of good necks. When we try to get a ewe-necked horse working correctly, we're fighting an uphill battle for we're fighting nature. The tendency towards ewe-necked horses should be completely eliminated from any future breeding programs.

A great many horses with proper necks are high-headed, or at least, throw their heads up when being handled or stopped. We must conclude that such horses have received poor training and are the result of reining a horse to hard stops over and over again. Actually, few horses stop correctly when pulled down from a hard gallop to a dead stop. The more this maneuver is practiced, the worse the fault becomes. Speed seems to be desired over correct work, and we'll have horses that stop with heads pointed skyward as long as speed is the criterion we judge reining classes by. Speed, brute force, high hands and stopping time after time make high-headed horses. When the horse is poorly handled, his natural head carriage will be much higher than that of the horse that has had correct work.

The high fork and horn of the western saddle forces the rider to hold his rein hand pretty high in order to work over such obstacles. "Low hands, low head. High hands, high head." This old axiom is certainly true. When the pull on the reins is *up*, the head goes up. When the pull on the reins is *back*, the head comes back, giving to

8

the bit rather than fighting it.

When the horse is pulled to a stop, the reins should be released so the horse can balance himself. If the reins are pulled and held tightly, the head will come in to some extent but the horse must soon resist the pull of the reins by throwing his head up to fight the pain. *For every action there is a reaction.* The reaction to a steady pull is resistance, the throwing of the head.

When stopping, the reins should be pulled, released and pulled again if the desired stop isn't sudden enough. The same thing applies when the horse is reined. There should be a slight give and take of the hands so that the horse never gets a real chance to set himself against the bit. Rein pressure should be light, off and on.

The matter of keeping the hands low is very important. The rein hand can be held in front of the fork with the reins coming from the bottom of the hand. Slack can be given by letting the reins slip a bit. The reins can be tightened by pulling the reins through the hand with the other hand. The reins may be held in the left hand and the rein ends, or romal may be held in the right hand. In this manner, the rein hand can rest continually on the horse's withers. When neck-reining a horse, no lower hand position is possible.

But, we must correct the high-headed horse. There are various devices that can be used for this purpose. The most common "gimmick" is the tie-down. A strap is run from the noseband of the bridle to the saddle cinch. The strap keeps the horse from throwing his head up — no cure is effected unless a painful object is used in place of the noseband. A piece of baling wire in lieu of the noseband will make head-tossing so painful that most horses will quit it. However, the habit may come back to them when the wire is removed. Use care, a scarred nose or even a broken nose can result from the use of a wire noseband.

A rope, chain or wire just back of the ears is often used. The chain and wire used in this fashion is a bit on the cruel side and their use should be confined to only the worst cases.

I don't care much for tie-downs. They are often fairly effective, but are very crude. Polo draw reins or a running martingale are more my style.

The Polo draw rein consists of two reins that run through a snaffle (colt) bit. They originate from a strap around the cinch, run between the horse's legs — through the bit to the rider. The pull is down and in. Most horses soon give to this rig. It is both sensible and moderate, and the animal is in no pain from this rig.

The running martingale serves the same purpose. Reins are run

The polo draw rein consists of two reins which originate from a strap around the cinch, run between the horse's legs, then through the bit to the rider. The pull is down and in.

through rings which make the pull as low as is desired. The end of the martingale is affixed to the cinch and runs between the horse's front legs. The strap has two ends with rings that the reins run through. Provision for change of length is made via a buckle.

The ultimate in good sense is to forget neck-reining and concentrate on getting a good headset. A rein is held in each hand and the rider can hold his hands as low as needed. The straight curb bit isn't used for this. A colt bit, Pelham, or Weymouth is the thing here.

Correcting high-headedness takes ten times longer than making the horses high-headed in the first place.

Barn Sour

The barn sour horse can be naturally so, or can be taught this bad habit. The "natural" is lazy, hungry or tired. He can be a stallion wanting to get back to his mares. He can be a colt wanting to get back to his friends. He can be an abused horse wanting to go back to the safety of his stall.

Most barn sour horses become so because they are allowed to come back to the barn at a run. Soon the run becomes *runaway*. When forced to walk back to the barn, the horse will pull, prance, dance, travel sideways, and when confirmed will rear and lunge in an effort to blindly get back to his home. Such a horse is a real mess.

The best way to get around owning a barn sour horse is to never let him get that way to start with. Always walk the horse the last part of the way to the barn. It's better to get soaking wet than to teach your horse to be barn sour.

If a horse has a lot of age, such a habit is almost impossible to cure. I have cured many horses of this bad habit.

Some horses rear straight up and lunge. One such horse was brought to me to correct. I saw that standard riding equipment was out the first time I tried him. I gave him the first round.

I equipped this horse with a colt bit, bit guard and draw reins. This particular bit guard is one of my own inventions and it insures against injury to the colt's mouth. I buckled on my spurs, dull ones, with silver dollars instead of rowells.

I rode this colt out into my arena and turned him towards the barn. When he gathered himself to rear and lunge, I pulled him into a spin with the draw reins and spurred him hard in the shoulder to keep him spinning and to show him that rearing hurt him.

When our dizziness ceased, I walked him towards the barn. He attempted to rear again and got the same treatment. After half a dozen "go-rounds," he travelled around the arena in good shape. After a few days, I rode him in the pasture. He tried me a few times and gave up this bad habit. I rode him for a few months and sent him back home, cured.

A fine Quarter horse gelding came to me for the same reason. Kids had repeatedly run him to the barn. Whenever he faced the barn, he squatted and jumped like a rope horse leaving the box. Different measures were in order.

This horse would respond to a colt bit so he was equipped with a colt bit and regular reins. I rode him into our largest arena, went to the far end and was determined to walk him to the barn on a loose rein. When he jumped towards the barn, I pulled him into a tight circle and let him run until he slowed, of his own accord, to a walk. This was accomplished by strong pulls and releases. This method will not work on a tight rein for the horse will lean into the bit and run

The Dave Jones Bit Guard is designed to vertically position the bit in the colt's mouth. By raising bit, colt can't get tongue over it. The bit is lowered as colt learns to carry it. Bit rings cannot hurt mouth when this guard is used.

until he drops.

When the horse dropped down to a walk, he was allowed to proceed towards the barn — on a loose rein. When he speeded up, he was pulled into the tight circle and allowed to travel at his own speed until he chose to drop down to a walk. He could then proceed to the barn.

After a few hours of such treatment, the horse finally realized the he *must* walk on a loose rein if he wanted to get to the barn. This procedure was repeated daily and the horse learned his lesson. He tried me a few times on pasture rides but found that walking from the pasture was just as necessary as walking from the arena.

Each horse requires a different mode of operation. There are many more ways of correcting the barn sour horse. Feed him away from the barn. Don't put him in his stall when the ride is over; tie him up a while, etc. Different horsemen will tell you different cures.

On the most stubborn, obstinate cases, I resort to throwing the

When the horse dropped down to a walk, he was allowed to proceed toward the barn on a loose rein. When he speeded up again, he was pulled into a tight circle.

horse and tying him down for some time. This is done humanely, on soft ground — and his legs are tied with soft ropes. Blankets are placed under his head to prevent injury. This has effected a cure on some of the worst horses I ever handled.

The Runaway — Stampeder

As Will James once said, the stampeder will make a cowboy "turn white around the gills." When a colt or a spoiled horse starts those wild lunges that mean *runaway*, his rider is in mortal danger. When a horse has learned that he can "stampede," it takes a real cowboy to convince him and to handle him.

The old time cowboy had one of the best cures. When a bronc stampeded, he'd "quit" him, throwing a leg over the horse's neck and would land on his heels, with a "mecate" (hackamore lead rope) locked over his hip. This would throw the bronc and the rider would tie him down for a few hours. The horse wanted no more of such stuff and would pay attention to his rider.

I'm not man enough for such action anymore. Few are, so we

In the regular draw rein arrangement, long latigo reins are attached to the cinch rings and run through the colt bit to the rider's hands.

resort to such stuff as draw reins. Any horse can be turned around with draw reins because they give the rider all the leverage.

Long, strong latigo reins are affixed to the cinch rings and run through the colt bit. Again my bit guard prevents injury to the colt's mouth. When the colt attempts to run away, he can be circled or doubled (jerked right around in his tracks). Caution!! If the horse is running wide open, he should be circled down to a stop rather than doubled for the abrupt double might throw him and the rider could be seriously injured. Double him before he gets started.

Rearing

Some horses rear naturally. If a horse is deep through the loin, with strong powerful buttocks, it's easy and natural for him to rear. The natural rearer can be discouraged by doubling or spinning him everytime he tries it. He does it because it's easy for him. He's not mean. A simple punishment will tell him that he shouldn't rear under saddle.

The horse that rears because he's mean — or one that has been taught to rear — is another matter. The danger in the rear is that a **14** horse may go straight up and fall over backwards on the rider.

I previously mentioned one method of breaking a horse of rearing. I used draw reins so I could pull him into a spin and re-enforced this by spurring him in the shoulder.

The old cowboy method of coping with a rearer was to pull him over backwards and then to tie him down. This is probably still the best method. However, rearing is a form of resistance and the trainer eventually effects a cure by punishing the horse after the action.

One day a mare named Kay reared straight up with me a dozen times. I am far too "chicken" to pull a horse over backwards so I got off, unsaddled, got a couple of foot ropes, tied up one hind leg, then tied up the other. Kay sat down. I pushed her on over and tied her down. I sacked her out with a slicker, and even shot a revolver around her before letting her up.

When she got up, I saddled her and rode off. Kay never reared again. She went on to win eight Western Pleasure classes in a row.

I will write more about *throwing* to correct a horse that has bad habits for it's the quickest, most humane method of disciplining a dangerous horse. However, the act of throwing a horse is, in itself, dangerous to the horse and to the person doing the throwing unless the person is very experienced, has correct equipment and proper facilities. If you have such a problem horse, I suggest professional help. If there's no experienced trainer in your locality, I suggest talking about the problem with your Veterinarian. He has proper equipment to throw a horse and he knows how to do it.

Sulking — Refusing To Move

Some colts resent being ridden and exhibit their temper by refusing to move. The rider who uses whip and spur excessively will make more than his share of sulkers. Getting a young horse too tired often has bad results. Starting a colt with little or no ground training may confuse him so much that he'll sulk in self-defense.

When sulking develops, the trainer should ask himself if he's moved too fast, worked the colt too long or skipped some necessary part of the initial training. He should then consider the colt. Does the colt have a narrow forehead and small eyes? It may be natural meanness in the colt and proper steps must be taken to compensate.

If the colt is a well-bred animal of good conformation, fine head and large mild eye, the trainer must consider the possibility of his own error. I would recommend that the trainer start over again from scratch.

The colt should be saddled with the stirrups hobbled (tied together under the animal) — long ropes or long lines should be 15

The colt should be saddled with the stirrups rigged high, and tied together under the animal so they won't flop. He will learn to turn, stop, start and back up before being ridden. However much time this training takes, it is time well spent.

affixed to the hackamore or colt bit and the colt should be driven until he again responds to signals to move out, stop and turn. If it takes a week to achieve good results, it's a week well spent. When the trainer decides to ride the colt, he should look for signs that could give him a clue to his previous trouble.

If the colt drives willingly but sulks when ridden — a tight saddle, not enough padding, dirty blankets, dirty cinch, latigos that rub or a sore back might be the culprit (culprits). The trainer should try a wider saddle accompanied by clean blankets and cinch. The colt's comfort could make the difference. I've seen clean, correct equipment solve many a problem.

The trainer should be careful not to hang on the colt's head. When starting a young horse, the reins are never held tightly. The colt is controlled by other means than a tight rein.

When a colt has a tendency to balk, it's a good idea to ride the colt with another horse. He's more apt to go along with the other horse than he is to balk.

But the trainer or the horse buyer will sometimes get "stuck" with
16   a balker and the confirmed sulking horse can be permanently cured

by only one sure-fired method. The spoiled sulker should be thrown and tied down.

A man brought me such a filly many years ago. This man had a rider working for him so bringing the filly to me was a bit peculiar. I was assured that she was green but gentle. I knew that I had a problem at the first saddling.

The filly stood quietly while I saddled and adjusted the hackamore. After leading her a few steps, I toed the stirrup and eased up. She stood quietly, never flicking an ear. After a few seconds, I tried to move her. Nothing. I pulled her this way and that. She still didn't move. Reaching behind her, I slapped her over the rump with my hand. She moved out and I had a pretty good ride.

Next day I tried her again. This time it took me five minutes before I could get her moving. As the days passed, she got progressively worse. She'd been started, spoiled, and as she became accustomed to her new home, reverted to her old ways. I phoned the owner, told him I had problems and that I wanted to see him.

The owner insisted that the filly hadn't been tampered with for he knew that trainers didn't like spoiled horses to work. From experience, I knew that he was lying to me, but I tried to be tactful. I said, "Mr. Smith, you brought me a valuable filly to train. She's a balker. The cure is pretty rough and I'd rather you'd be present in case she might be injured. You can take her home and there'll be no further charge or I can work on her, cure her and go on and train her."

Mr. Smith replied, "She's sure no good like she is. Work on her!"

I rigged the filly to drive and slapped her on the rump with a longing whip. She threw herself over backwards as sulkers are prone to do. We held her down and I tied her legs. Then I sacked her out with my slicker. We took turns rubbing her and lightly slapping her. I was in no hurry to let her get up.

Finally, I untied the foot ropes and she lunged to her feet. I adjusted the cinch, stepped on and rode away. She was all right from then on.

So, if you have such a horse — a confirmed sulker, and you're somewhat inexperienced, I suggest calling your Veterinarian. He can throw the horse for you and tie it down. The horse should be down at least an hour to effect a cure. Please don't try this yourself if you don't know how.

Shying Horses

It's very provoking to ride a horse that's continually spooking from one side of the trail to the other; jumping at every stump and root.

When this filly threw herself over backwards, as some sulkers are prone to do, she was held down and her legs were tied. She was then sacked out with a slicker and lightly rubbed all over before she was allowed to regain her feet.

It can be dangerous for the novice rider because many people can't stay with the sudden jump when the horse shies. The horse that jumps ten feet sideways can unseat a good rider.

Horses often fall when they spook. I was once riding in a heavy snow in Nebraska. The filly I was on was extremely nervous and flighty, a condition we later found to be caused by cystic ovaries. We were travelling up a rocky, steep trail on the way to check mares on a meadow.

Rounding a turn, we surprised a huge buck deer that jumped and ran. The filly jumped so violently that she fell on her side, pinning my leg under her. When she scrambled up, my right foot was hung up in the stirrup.

Many horses would have wheeled, kicked me and dragged me. The filly was so scared she was petrified. Humped up, snorting, she backed a few steps and stopped. I eased toward her a bit and wiggled my foot. She snorted and ran back but still didn't bolt. Finally, I inched my way on my back until I could get some slack and wiggled loose. I grabbed a dragging rein and had my horse. Mounting, I rode on to search for the mares. After about fifteen minutes, I started to shake with fear, for my close shave gradually dawned on me.

Young horses spook. They do so with no human near them. It's part of a horse's make-up to spook, jump and run. A colt will invent things to spook it. Cows do this. I imagine all animals do. I'm so used to riding horses that spook that I tense up and get ready for "my horse" to jump if a piece of paper blows in front of me when I'm on foot walking down a city street.

When we want a horse *not* to spook, we're asking the horse to behave unnaturally. Punishing a horse for shying just doesn't work because the horse associates pain with the object which made him spook. Punishing him only makes him more frightened.

If a horse is fed a lot of grain, he'll have surplus energy to work off, and will be far more prone to spook, jump and run than he would be on a more moderate ration. The people who really have their problems are "week-end" riders, people who work all week and hope to ride for pleasure on the week-end. Their horses have been standing around all week storing up energy like a battery. When the rider saddles up, the horse is apt to go off like a bomb.

Perhaps the horse could be turned out for awhile to run and get some of that energy drained off. A better plan would be to allow the horse to run in and out of a pasture all week where he can take whatever work he feels like. He'll then be much safer to ride.

Arena work, some good hard trotting, especially in deep sand, is a good prelude to a trail ride. A half-hour of arena work might keep the week-end rider out of the hospital.

Some horses, like people, have poor vision. Any sort of movement will frighten such a horse because he can't tell whether a flapping sheet is a flapping sheet or a Polar bear jumping out to get him.

A horse's eyesight is different from a person's. A horse has no depth perception up close for he sees close objects with one eye at a time. He can't focus on close objects so the hand that reaches out to stroke the colt's muzzle may trigger a front hoof that strikes like a snake. This is no fault of the colt. One must understand these things about horses.

Many breeds of horses are naturally more flighty than other breeds. Arabians and Pasos, for instance, have for centuries worked day-in and day-out. These breeds have become noted for their endurance. Take such a horse, put him in a stall, feed him huge quantities of grain and he'll go "stir-crazy." A half hour's work only makes him want more. Of course, a horse with all this bottled up energy won't be gentle.

Horses can be trained to accept most spooky objects they see without shying if they're given a strict training program that includes

If a horse should shy, ride him up to the spooky object, forcing him there with voice and legs. He'll snort and blow, but will want to smell it. Repeat until fear is gone.

plenty of exercise. Imagine what the horses of the New York Police Department must put up with. Granted, not all horses will settle down enough to make police mounts but enough of them do to prove that we can take almost any horse and get the spook out of it.

First, we start by riding the animal enough to get the raw edge off. After a week of good hard exercise, you'll be surprised at how much less your horse shies.

When he does shy, ride him up to the spooky object, forcing him up with voice and legs. If he refuses, a "popper" might be necessary to get him to the object of his fear. He'll snort and blow but will want to smell it. Let him do this. The horse will then noticeably relax. Pet him and reward him with something he likes to eat when this is practical. Ride away and return to the spooky object. He may shy a bit but will be much easier to force up the next time. Repeat until 20 he no longer has any fear.

This "de-spooking" can be continued until the horse shies at nothing. Trail horses must accept the unacceptable and their trainers constantly work at getting them used to everything. I've seen trail horses in training stand on bearskins to eat their grain. Standing on a cowhide is also very common, as is standing in water. Quite often, such horses get fed in their trailers to make certain they'll eagerly jump in when asked. With food as a reward, a horse will accept almost anything.

Kicking

A horse that kicks is a dangerous animal. Most horses kick when startled so it's a good idea to talk, whistle or sing when walking behind horses. Many horses are cranky about their food and will kick a person if bothered when feeding. Feed them and leave them alone until they've finished. Mares may kick when zealously guarding their offspring. Colts may kick because they've never been shown that they shouldn't. The person who associates with horses must certainly be on guard. Even then, the top horseman will occasionally get kicked. I have been hurt many times by kicking horses and have had near misses that could have maimed or killed me. However, I firmly believe that the housewife who drives her children to and from school is in far more danger from traffic than I am from horses. I've had whistling hooves miss my head by a foot but we pass that close to mechanized destruction every time we meet a car on the road.

The horse that kicks from meanness must be disciplined at the time of the infraction. The horse handler should carry some form of whip and punish the horse immediately — *when* he kicks, not after. I favor a double latigo because a "popper" makes a loud noise, but actually inflicts little pain. It *scares* the meanness out of them.

A horse that kicks at other horses in the ring or on the trail is a different problem for it's far more dangerous to discipline a horse when you're riding him. The method is the same. The horse should be whipped for this bad habit at the time of the infraction. It might be wise for the novice to take the horse to a professional for correction, because —

(1) When riding a kicking horse, you must whip the animal for kicking and, in doing so, might cause the kicker to run away. If you're not SURE that you can control your horse, take him to a professional. Don't get hurt!

(2) The occasional cranky devil that kicks in spite of all punishment (correction) should be subdued. He should be thrown and tied down. ■

CHAPTER THREE

WHY AND HOW A HORSE IS THROWN

A fellow once criticized my writing. He said, "Jones has one cure for everything. He just throws a bronc and ties it down. That's all he knows."

The man wasn't quite right. I seldomly throw a horse, while there are many trainers who throw all of them. Some guys dump a colt with a "running W" for the least little mistake. I don't believe in this. I tie down "rank ones" — bad horses — for it's far more humane than beating on them.

Professor Rarey, the famous English horse tamer, deplored the constant beating of horses in his country. He knew that beating a horse for a minor fault often turned the animal into a man-hater. There had to be a better way and he explored until he found it.

Rarey was badly injured many times but considered getting hurt an occupational hazard. A horse might bite, strike or kick him while he'd be getting the training bridle, surcingle and foot ropes on the outlaw. Once the animal was thrown and tied down, his troubles ceased.

The professor rationalized that a horse has two reasons for self-protection — FIGHT and FLIGHT. He can fight his tormentor or he can run away from him. If the horse can neither fight nor escape, he will soon surrender. He will accept man's dominance. He will realize that this puny creature can make him helpless, and will become a different animal when allowed to regain his feet.

When I was a child, I heard that a vicious horse could be subdued by beating him until he moaned. That meant surrender. Many old time horsemen would throw a horse and beat him until he was half dead and I suppose such goings-on are still practiced. This is *totally unnecessary*. A horse never needs to be punished when he's tied down. I go all over the horse with a *light* slapping motion, blow in his nostrils and even flap a light raincoat all over him. I'll roll him over and do both sides. The surface of the breaking pen is soft to avoid injury to the eye. The horse will struggle for awhile but will eventually give up to calmly lie there. He can then be released. When the treatment is done, the trainer should reward the horse with a bit of food, some kind words and petting.

This treatment is very nerve-wracking for the horse — very up-setting — so care should be taken not to do this right after, or soon after feeding. Nervousness will upset a person's stomach and it can colic a horse. The horse should be walked, then noticed for the rest of the day. A traumatic experience can result in colic.

The problem horse is generally corrected by throwing and tying him down ONCE. There is no reason why you should not have your Veterinarian do this for you since he has a casting harness and knows how to use it. He must throw horses many times a year for various reasons so he's practiced at it.

There are various methods of throwing horses. The Veterinarian uses a casting harness. Buckles with rings are affixed to the hind pasterns. Ropes run from a neck collar to the rings and back up through the collar. The ropes are pulled and the horse is forced to sit down. He's then rolled over and tied down.

One method I use is to Scotch hobble one hind leg, then go to the other side and Scotch up the other hind leg. The horse sits down. Since the hind legs are already pulled up, the horse finds it impossible to kick. This is a fairly safe method. A very good way to secure the horse after he's been thrown is to hobble the front and rear leg on each side, and if necessary, tie the hobbles together. Extra-strong hobbles should be used for this purpose.

Invariably someone asks, "What do you do when the colt is too wild to hobble in any manner?"

I continue to hope that I'll not be forced to deal with such wild horses. However, I have often had this problem to cope with. Let's say that we have a very wild, strong two-year old to gentle.

When a chute and snubbing post are available, I run the colt into the chute, halter him and tie a long soft rope around his neck with a non-slip bowline knot. The rope runs through the halter, the colt is released from the chute and runs around the pen. The trainer works him to the snubbing post. A helper spooks the colt up fairly close and the rope is wrapped and tied off. Both men move away from the colt to give him time to understand that he can't get away from the post. The trainer soon attempts to touch the colt and to feed him a few bites of grain to let him know there's no need to be wild. The men gradually rub all over the colt — brush him, etc. When the colt stands well for all this, he can be easily blindfolded and hobbled. The front-leg hobbles and a side-line are generally used at this time. The colt can stand with no discomfort but can't kick or run away. He would fall if he tried.

A horse has two ways to protect himself — fight or flight! If he can do neither, he will soon surrender and accept man's dominance. While there are various methods used to throw horses, it is obvious that it is no job for a novice. The problem horse is generally corrected by going through this experience just one time, and your Veterinarian is the individual you should call upon to get the job done because he knows how to do it. He has a casting harness and uses it to throw horses many times every year.

But some colts, being individuals, are very wild, rank, and must be subdued. After months of handling, such colts remain rank unless they're thrown and tied down. For instance:

A man pulled into a horse farm I managed and wanted four yearlings. He had to load up and move out in a few hours. One filly was very rank.

We had haltered this filly in a chute and had broken her to lead. Meanwhile, we'd been very busy and had had no chance to go on with her training.

We drove the filly into the chute, got a rope tied around her neck, let her out and got her snubbed to the post. Then we were stuck because the filly screamed and struck viciously every time we approached. Gentling seemed a matter of months rather than hours.

But the filly had to be gentled immediately. Blindfolding her was necessary. I tried flopping a big horse blanket over her head but those front hooves took it away from me every time. And every time she pawed it, the blanket went down under her and was very dangerous to retrieve. Finally it caught in the wraps of the rope on the snubbing post and I managed to flip the rest of it over her head. She calmed down immediately.

I brought up a soft-braided, cotton rope and snared her front legs in a figure-eight. Then we released her from the post. She made one lunge and I threw her. My helper dropped on her head to hold her down while I tied her legs. We then spent fifteen minutes rubbing her and flapping the old raincoat all over her. When we allowed her to get up, she was a different filly.

Before we had the chute, I had to forefoot, throw and tie down wild colts just to get hold of them. This was hard work and somewhat dangerous to both horses and trainer. Forefooting to throw a colt is often done and is all right when done by experts. ■

CHAPTER FOUR

CURES FOR BAD MANNERS

Many equine bad manners are caused by inept training or poor riders. But it would be unfair to always blame the human because some horses seem to be naturally prone to them.

Striking, Biting And Nipping

While kicking is often a horse's grouchy retort to being bothered or frightened, striking and biting are more associated with the wild or mean horse. The bronc will strike hard and accurately; he'll bite to kill or maim. These problems are seldom encountered in colts that are hand-raised. There is a great cure for the vicious horse. He should be thrown, tied down and subdued before he kills someone.

The horse that nips is a more common problem. I say "nip" rather than "bite" — though both are bites. The horse that nips may be a bit mean or cranky but he's not trying to kill a person.

Nipping is a trait of stallions and of colts that are fed by hand. Giving a horse tid-bits such as sugar can lead to nipping. I don't say not to feed horses by hand for I do it all the time. I do say to stop it if the horse starts nipping.

Many people fool around with a stallion so long that he gets irked and nips. Maybe he'll nip when being cleaned up, while having his hooves cleaned, or when being cinched up. Most experts advise having a board with a nail in it ready. When the horse reaches around to nip, he hits the nail and punishes himself. Since punishment should be accomplished the second the horse tries to nip, this method does work.

Another good method is to make a little halter with a piece of baling wire for a noseband. The wire should be snug but not extremely tight. When the horse tries to bite his handler, the wire bites him back.

The most common method of correcting the nipping horse is to carry a "popper" or some other type of short whip. When the horse tries to bite, he's whopped for it.

A line-bred horse is often nervous. A colt such as this was brought to me for training. The colt was a wonder to train but was so soft he had to be walked after each little ride. He was so bad about nipping that a boy who worked for me told me he'd quit rather than walk that "so and so" one more time.

I walked the colt myself after the next ride. My weapon was a "popper" — a length of double latigo. I used this because the colt would fight back if whipped. The sting of a training whip would make him strike and bite — make him worse. The popper doesn't hurt. It makes a loud noise, but there's no real pain connected with its use.

The colt nipped at me and I hit him as hard as I could, once, along his shoulders. It sounded like a gun going off. He jumped back in his astonishment. When we resumed our walk, he made no further attempts to nip. My helper then started carrying the popper when he walked the colt and had no more trouble with him.

Bad Trail And Show Ring Manners

I previously discussed horses that kick at other horses when being ridden. You remember that I said that the offending horse should be whipped for his bad manners when he tried his kicking. I also said that it was dangerous to whip a horse while riding him because doing so might result in a runaway. I suggested professional help rather than taking the chance of getting hurt.

Now we should talk about other bad show and trail manners. How about the horse that speeds up, wanting to run through horses to get to the head of the bunch? The act is both dangerous and annoying. Speed has "come down" on such a horse. He wants to run, must be fought to get slowed down and generally prances along, lugging at the bit and throwing his head to get it free to run some more. The horse must be slowed down and taught to walk.

Many people let their horses run to the barn. I always walk my colt or horse to the barn. If this is done every day, the horse knows that he MUST walk if he wants to get back. When I trail ride with other horses, I seldom run mine, preferring to cover ground at a walk or a trot. If I do lope, it's always in the direction away from the barn. I've heard people say that they wouldn't own a horse if they had to be that careful. Such people generally have spoiled horses. I'm careful because I'm a trainer and want to teach my horse how to work and give him good, not bad habits.

Holding-in a horse seldom works. Such a horse seems better able to figure it out if he works a loose rein for he'll lean into a tight rein and run until he drops. Working on a loose rein, never neckreining — running in circles until the horse slows of his own accord, is one of the best answers.

28   What if the rider can't turn the horse? Draw reins greatly help

Draw reins greatly help the rider with the horse that won't turn. The leverage is greatly increased, and the horse can be painlessly shown that he CAN be turned by his rider.

the rider with the horse that won't turn. The rein is fastened onto the cinch ring, runs through the bit ring, and then to the rider. Leverage is greatly increased. Again, use a bit guard to avoid injury to the colt's mouth. The horse can be painlessly shown that he CAN be turned, and then he can be taught to circle on a loose rein.

Circling always helps slow a horse down. If a pleasure horse lopes too fast, he can be circled until he slows down and then allowed to resume his large circle of the ring. If he again speeds up, go back to small circles.

Sometimes the colt will work perfectly by himself but will charge-up when worked with other horses. Naturally, the horse can't be circled at a horse show, but show conditions can be simulated at home. Ask some friends over to practice. When your horse speeds up in the company of other horses, slow him down with small circles. Don't ask him to immediately turn into a top horse after a few circles. Chances are, many practice sessions with the other horses will be necessary before you notice much improvement. Good horse training consists of first finding out the correct procedure, and then drilling the correct method over and over until the horse's bad habit is eliminated. Many people enjoy watching the horse gradually develop into a fine working animal. These people make good trainers.

There are many places on the trail where it's impossible to make the colt lope in small circles. The rider has no choice but to hold the colt in until a place is found that will do for circling work. It's actually better to keep the colt at home until he's learned to slow down. What will work for the show horse will generally work for the trail horse. The problem is the same. The horse just wants to run through to get to the head of the pack.

Hard To Shoe Horses

Horse owners are usually the ones who make life tough for farriers, not the horses. We all tend to be far too lazy about cleaning our horse's hooves every day. This can be a matter of routine when a person rides one horse, but when a trainer rides eight a day, he's looking for all the shortcuts he can take.

Perhaps the horse, as a colt, was trained well and could have his hooves picked up, cleaned and trimmed with no problem. Then, one day his owner decided to clean his hooves at feeding time. The colt, grouchy at being disturbed, takes a little kick at the man. Next day, the man subconsciously forgets to clean the colt's hooves. Later, the colt senses that the man fears him and his habit becomes worse. Soon, he's taking a swat at anyone who comes near. When the colt's hooves need trimming, the man calls his farrier. The farrier comes out, catches the colt (owner is conveniently absent) and finds that the colt is pretty mean to handle. This gives the farrier several choices. He can chastise the colt and hope that this works. He can use restraining gear. He can load up his equipment and leave. Today, the shoer will generally pack up and leave. If he attempts to punish the colt for kicking, someone may see him and label him "mean." This could be the end of his career as a farrier.

On the other hand, some farriers *will* abuse a horse that doesn't stand well and long enough. He wants horses to stand as still as a statue, putting a little, but not too much weight on him. He can shoe this perfect horse and move on to shoe more perfect horses. Horses that are easy to shoe allow him to finish quickly and move on to make more money. A fighting horse costs him time and money. Perhaps shoers should charge more for unruly horses and spend more time with them. Many farriers definitely need to be more patient with younger horses. How can we help our farriers and the horses that he works on for us?

First, we should pick up and clean our horse's hooves every day. It is also good to hold the hooves in the same position the shoer does. It's a good idea to tap on them to simulate the farrier nailing shoes on. If the horse misbehaves, we should punish him for it. On the other hand, we should reward him for standing quietly.

If the horse is very bad about his hooves, professional help should be sought. The pro will tie up a hind hoof, take the foot rope off, handle the legs and reprimand the horse if he doesn't cooperate.

When I have a "raw" bronc to handle, I'll hobble the front legs and sideline one hind leg. I will rub all the legs. The colt can't kick me with three of his legs tied; can't run away and will punish himself by falling if he attempts anything wild. He soon learns to stand quietly. I'll pick up the free hind leg. When he allows me to handle this leg, I'll sideline the gentle leg and handle the one previously sidelined. When he's gentle with his hind hooves, I'll remove the hobbles plus the sideline. Then I'll handle the front hooves. If he's unruly about them. I'll strap up each one until he behaves. He'll soon stand quietly to have all of his hooves handled.

Next day, I'll take no chances. The colt will be hobbled and sidelined before I handle the hooves. He'll be much gentler than the first day. He'll progress each day. Soon, I'll forget the hobbles and start handling the hooves as a farrier would. If I have any setbacks, I'll go back to the hobbles and sideline.

This method is almost foolproof, and is much better than whipping a horse. Whipping a horse only makes him fear shoeing. If a horse acts silly when he should know better, I'll slap him with the flat of my hand and yell at him. This tells him that I'm displeased. Really whipping him only makes him dread the farrier. It's like going to a dentist. If a dentist hurts us once, we'll always dread going back.

Please remember that when I discuss hobbling, sidelining, tying up a hoof or throwing a horse, such activity is *always* carried on in a breaking pen with soft ground, sand, shavings, or other soft material used as footing, so that the horse won't be injured. There is always the chance that the horse may be injured under the best circumstances. Don't work with poor conditions.

Grouch Horses

Yes, there are grouchy horses. Some ponies purchased for small children personify this problem. A man buys a pony for a small child. The child hasn't the strength to use the pony. The pony eats grass when he wants too, often pulling the child out of the saddle when he

When a horse is kicky, he can be hobbled and side-lined. Then the free hoof is picked up. After handling this leg, the side-line is changed to the other leg and process repeated.

jerks the ole' head down to the green stuff. Little can be done about this because the pony is too small for a man to ride. If a man does ride and correct the pony, the pony knows that the child can't control him when he tries to next time. Ponies have a bad reputation because of this. It's a tough problem.

We have the same sort of problem with a mare that's boarding here. Her owner is a small girl. The mare bucked the girl off many times before she was put in training. When I rode her, the mare made a feeble attempt to buck with me. She found that such stuff was not wise — pronto! She worked better day by day. She worked pretty good for the girl as long as she was in training. When the mare was put on board, she reverted to her original way of going. The mare is for sale. She's been replaced by a small willing mare that never does a bad thing and wants to be ridden. The girl is very pleased with her new horse.

I imagine that this situation is very prevalent. A horse will realize that the owner can't make him do anything. The horse is sent to a trainer and the problem is "duck soup," or no problem at all. The trainer works the horse. The horse knows that it must work. The owner sees the result and is very pleased. The horse comes home and bucks off his owner. The only real solution is a change of horses. The first horse will be a good one for anyone who can *make* him work. Then, if the first owner can replace the horse with one that wants to do right, everyone is happy.

It's very possible that the first horse I talked about wasn't ridden well enough or long enough by the professional who started the job. Thus, we have a beginner (rider) on a half-trained filly. Good habits are pushed aside by bad habits and a semi-spoiled horse is the result. The horse that only works because it has to — is most certainly a grouch.

Horses are often made grouchy by rough trainers who work them too hard and too long. Then the young horse is irritated with its rider and become ill-natured. Get a young one too tired and it will resent being ridden. Knock on one too much and ill temper is the inevitable result. I would turn such a horse out to pasture for quite a few months and re-start it, being kind and giving it no really long rides that might get it too tired.

Sometimes a young horse will get a "crush" on its trainer. The trainer gives the colt its food and exercise. Soon, the colt resents anyone else trying to handle it. The trainer should have other trainers switch-off on the colt when possible. One-man horses can easily be made and this doesn't set too well with the owner when he gets his colt back home. I like to have a good rider working with me whenever possible and this is one of the main reasons for having another rider on the payroll.

The Bucking Horse

There are bucking horses — and then there are *bucking* horses. The really rank horse that puts all the local talent down has a place to go. His home should be rodeo. That's the way they like them.

Then there are the horses that just buck enough to be a problem. A horse, feeling good, bucks his owner down. The owner sustains a slight injury and doesn't ride the horse for a few days. Next time, it's "empty saddles" again. The owner now definitely fears the horse. Riding is no pleasure. Chances are, if the horse had some of his surplus energy worked off, he'd never have bucked. Putting his timid rider down started to fix the bucking habit.

How do you cure it? The horse just needs some miles put on him by someone who can ride him. He might *try* a new rider but if that rider can stay aboard, the horse should forget the previous incident. A few months riding would straighten out the problem.

Horses are unpredictable. We all have the tendency to think that once a horse is well trained, he'll just go on functioning forever. But horses, like people, have feelings and a horse might buck simply because he feels like it.

A cow ranch in the southeast owned a horse named Lollar. Lollar, a gelding, was about as good an all-round cowhorse as I ever rode. Anyone could ride him. He'd do a good job cutting cattle; he was strong enough to hold a bull, and he was a good enough rope horse to hold his own in a calf roping contest. He did little jobs of work every day, was kept in the cow barn, fed the best and got along with everyone.

One morning, the ranch's top cowboy stepped up on Lollar, started out to check pastures and Lollar bucked him off into a pile of rocks. This rider was no slouch. He'd entered many a rodeo and had won his share of the loot riding rough stock. Of course, Lollar completely surprised him and that was most of it. No one remembered that Lollar ever bucked before or after this incident.

A young girl owned a nice Quarter horse filly and brought her to board at Meridian Meadows. How a boarder handles his horse is his own business so I didn't pay much attention to the goings-on for some time. I finally noticed that the girl spent a lot more time lunging than she did riding. It was easy to see why. The filly would buck for fifteen minutes after being saddled. She layed her ears back and seemed ill at ease when ridden. The girl would come out often to work this filly, but she was deathly afraid of her. She'd wanted a horse, found this one and talked her parents into buying it for her. She really didn't want to work the filly but thought that she owed it to her parents.

One day I talked to the girl about her horse, asking her if she didn't think it a good idea to have us work the filly for her until she was better trained. The girl thought that this was an excellent idea and asked me if I'd talk to her parents about it. I did and they agreed. They didn't know that their daughter was so afraid of her horse.

Before starting the chore, I looked the situation over thoroughly. The filly was round-backed. Their saddle certainly wasn't made for a round-backed horse. She, and her parents, being novices, had purchased a cheap new saddle that came nowhere near fitting the animal. It pinched her which caused her to act so badly. If pinchy-shoes hurt, imagine how a bad-fitting saddle feels.

Before telling the people about it, I decided to test my theory.

A filly comes "unglued." The rider had no trouble staying on board and used a popper to slap the buck out of her. After correction she never again attempted to buck.

Using a very wide saddle, I rigged and led her into the arena. During saddling, the filly had ears layed back. When I mounted, she danced around a bit with a wild expression on her face, but soon settled down and gave me a good ride. She was much better the next day. After a week, the filly enjoyed being ridden.

I told the people that I'd found the key. The girl came out, watched me ride and then rode the filly. She seemed pleased, came out a few times to ride but ended up selling the filly. She had lost all interest in horses. Though her filly was made safe by the selection of proper gear, she still entertained a dread of her and, by fearing her filly, feared all horses.

There are bucking horses actually bred to buck. Some ranchers raise bucking horses for rodeos. None of these horses are meant for use as saddle horses. Almost all bucking horses are made that way by their owners, and ignorance is usually the big factor.

I've had my share of bucking horses. I'll try to knock the buck

Hackamore reins are snugged up and filly is turned loose in breaking pen. If she tries to buck, the action will cause the hackamore to rap her sharply.

out of a bronc with my "popper." The loud "whack" seems to do more good than a quirt does to discourage the habit. The loud noise and the slap seem to frighten the horse out of his tendency to buck. The pain of a whip will often make the horse fight more.

A man once brought a colt of little value to me. He had to have the colt broken in order to sell him and he didn't want to put much money in him. We made a deal on some money and some hay.

I later found out that the colt had been started and spoiled by the owner. Different "bronc riders" had tried him and all of them had been put down. The man told me nothing about this.

The colt was easy to saddle and mount. He walked right away and trotted out in good shape. When I pushed him into a lope he "broke in two." He wasn't all that hard to ride. I finally pulled him up and got my popper. When he bucked the next time, I tried to knock it out of him, but had no luck. This colt pulled his head right down on the ground, bellowed, bucked and got worse the more I whipped him. Different methods seemed to be called for.

The colt always dropped his head clear down to the ground to buck. This was a clue. I had to show him that I didn't want him to buck, plus I wanted to make the act of dropping his head somewhat painful.

I have a hackamore that I used twenty years ago on coarse broncs. It's stiff and very heavy; too much hackamore for good horses. This is what I put on him.

When the colt dropped his head, I put all I had into pulling that head up and spinning him around. In doing so, I scraped a few inches of hair off of his jaw but I got that big ugly head up. It really scared him! He cantered around a little, keeping his eye on me. After that, a light pull was enough to make him be good. He got kind words and much petting when he was good. His owner was very pleased.

Remember:

If a horse has a good head and a mild eye, he won't have a tendency towards bucking.

A horse left to run wild until he is three or four years of age will be much wilder than the animal that's been hand-raised. A good colt which has known humans from his first day will seldom buck.

Horses that have little exercise and too much feed will be inclined to buck. Horses store up energy like a battery does power. Charging up the horse with feed is like charging up the battery. They're READY. Drain off the horse's surplus energy with exercise, preferably before riding him.

A saddle that doesn't fit hurts the horse. He can't say "the saddle hurts my back" so he must *show* his owner that he's in pain. One way to do this is to buck. I'd rather pad a too-wide saddle with extra blankets than take a chance on one that might be too narrow.

When a novice has a horse that has developed the bucking habit, the horse should be sent to a professional for re-training. Bucking is dangerous. Even if a novice can ride the storm out, nothing is being done to cure the bad habit.

When all else fails, rank bucking horses should be subdued by throwing and tying them down. Remember, *please,* this is a job for a professional horseman or Veterinarian. ■

CHAPTER FIVE

BAD EXPERIENCES AND THEIR REMEDIES

Some problems seem to directly relate to a specific experience, or to a series of events. Whether or not they could have been prevented by the use of better equipment, or through the employment of a more knowledgeable horsemanship, is quite beside the point. The problem has developed and it must now be dealt with.

Cinchy And Hard To Saddle Horses

I don't believe I ever *made* a horse "cinchy." However, I have had many brought to me with this problem. Most of them gradually got better. Some were real dillies!

A man buys a round-backed horse. He notices that when he gets ready to ride that his saddle wants to roll around. He pulls the cinch much tighter, too tight, and the horse humps his back, runs backward and then falls over backwards. The horse is bewildered by the choking effect of the too-tight cinch, and produces this action as a result. Some horses are much more sensitive than others.

Solution? A saddle that fits; preferably, one that is rigged in the skirts, so the saddle is really cinched on low down. Such a saddle sort of wraps around a horse and will stay on without cinching it too tight.

Getting a horse over his fright is a bit of a problem. He should be cinched only enough to keep the saddle in place, led a few steps, cinched a little tighter, etc., until the saddle is snug enough to stay on for the ride. The horse can be saddled, bridled, with the reins tied up, and turned into a pen. I used to do this while I cleaned the horse's stall. After five minutes, the saddle was cinched a bit tighter. When the stall was cleaned and bedded down, the colt was ready to ride. Cinching up a saddle that *fits right* is the answer to a "cinchy" colt.

Hard to saddle horses are made so by people who are careless when saddling. Many folks think it looks "western" to sort of throw the saddle on a horse. After that off stirrup hits the horse on the elbow a few times, the horse will become hard to saddle.

Other people tie up the cinch and off stirrup, go around and lower them. If the horse is a bit "antsy," he'll move or jump when

Correct fit! A wide saddle for a wide horse! If a saddle is too wide, the fork rides right on the withers and is extremely painful if ridden. A too-narrow saddle is unstable.

This is how a saddle is eased on a colt. Everything is lowered gently into place. If
horses are always saddled like this, very little trouble will develop.

the person walks around to the off side. The saddle will fall off. When it falls, the horse will jump back. This will teach him to throw himself backwards when being saddled.

I'm fairly tall. I realize the problem that a short person has when saddling a horse. Perhaps the very short person should have help when saddling a tall horse. Why is it that short people always ride great big horses?

Over the years, I learned how to put a saddle on a horse. It's hard to explain. The right hand holds the cinch and the off stirrup. The whole thing is eased onto the colt's back. The cinch almost always drops correctly and needs no immediate checking. I reach under to get the cinch and then lightly secure the saddle. Then I check to make sure everything is in the right place.

After the horse has been spoiled, flying backward everytime the saddle is brought near him, correction is difficult. I will thoroughly train the horse to hobbles, take him to the breaking pen and saddle him there. I'll put that saddle on and take it off him for an hour. When he finds that this doesn't hurt, he'll be on the way to being a horse that's easy to saddle. Only time and patience will overcome such a bad habit.

Many people around the world use blindfolds for saddling. This is sometimes a last resort so one shouldn't give up until a blindfold is tried. Remember to try to better the horse. A blindfold may make him easy to saddle but it teaches him very little. He has to see what's going on to learn anything.

Halter Pullers

We are all too familiar with halter pullers. Horses are made that way by being tied up, startled and breaking loose when they jump back. After a horse learns to do this, he can become dangerous to himself and people around him for he'll try to break loose at the slightest excuse.

This is partly the fault of the halters we're forced to buy. Most horses can break a leather halter. Nylon halters may seem a good solution but manufacturers often use such cheap hardware on them that they'll take no pull at all.

However, it might be best if the confirmed puller isn't tied with something he can't break for he may break or kink his neck. We almost never tie a colt up with an unbreakable halter. The preferred method is to tie a strong soft rope around his neck with a bowline knot and then to run the rope through the halter. He's not nearly as apt to hurt himself if the pull is farther back on his neck. He's tied **41** to a snubbing post and learns that he can't get away when he pulls back.

A method of breaking the halter-pulling habit is to tie a soft rope (bowline knot) around the horse's girth, then run the rope through the halter to the snubbing post. The rope holds the whole horse, causes discomfort when the horse pulls back and teaches him not to pull back. I recommend such a rig in every case. There are a few other technical methods used to teach a horse not to pull back. In each case, they are for the professional and I can see little to recommend them over the aforementioned method.

Hard To Haul Horses

Working on a horse ranch, I had to load a great many colts that had never before seen a truck or trailer. Many had almost no previous handling. Almost all of them went on very easily. This convinced me that people cause the problems with hard to load and hard to haul horses.

Cheap little trailers are a big hazard. If the horse is wedged into a little trailer with no room to move his legs or to raise his head, he's going to suffer on a long haul. He certainly won't want to get into that trailer again. If he bangs his head, he won't want to repeat. If the driver is continually standing him on his head when he stops and throws him off balance when he turns, the horse will dread being hauled.

To appreciate what a horse goes through, ride in a trailer while someone drives across a pasture (it's illegal for a person to ride in a trailer on the road), stopping and turning as he normally would in traffic. Try to ride, keeping your balance, without holding on. You'll see how impossible it is.

Now have the driver give you a slight signal (touching the brakes) before stopping. You then have a chance to prepare yourself. Have him touch the brakes lightly before turning. When the driver turns slowly, it's much easier. In this way, you can see what a difference a compassionate driver makes.

I used to haul my old roping mare, Fleetwing, in a three-quarter ton truck. She had a lot of room and loved her stall on wheels. Fleetwing would go in the truck if she could get to it. It had a high ceiling, an eight foot bed and plenty of width. At one rodeo, she was frightened by jets from a nearby air base. I had to allow her to stay in the truck because she felt secure there.

Forcing a horse to load isn't a good idea but it's often necessary.
42 Two men can clasp hands behind a gentle colt and manhandle him

To break the halter-puller, tie a soft rope (bowline knot) around the horse's girth, then run the rope through the halter to a snubbing post.

onto a trailer. Crossed ropes behind the horse will load most of them. Loading from a chute into a trailer or stock truck is almost foolproof. The trailer can back to a runway or stall where some wild motion behind the colt will force him to load, accepting the lesser of two evils.

To really have a good loading horse, park the trailer in his run, block it up and put feed in it. When he discovers that he can eat by going in the trailer, he'll soon love it.

What happens after the horse is loaded determines what kind of a hauling horse he'll make. If he likes what happens to him on that trailer, he'll load readily. If he has had bad experiences, he'll dread the trailer.

Once, in Colorado, a spotted mare was hauled in with a load of cattle to be bred to a paint stud the outfit owned. This mare was old and rank. She was bred by being turned out with the stud. The problem, after she settled, was how to load and haul her back to her owner.

I watched the attempts made and said nothing. She caved in the top of the trailer by rearing and striking. When my advice was asked for, I said that she should be thrown and tied down, for experience **43**

Forcing a horse to load isn't a good idea, but it's often necessary. Crossed ropes behind the horse will load most of them.

has shown me that old wild horses need stern measures. She was tied down for a few hours. When we let her get up, she meekly entered the trailer and was no trouble to haul.

Remember how to drive after the horse is loaded. Please don't jam a big horse into a little trailer. Most trailers are too small for the horses they carry.

The Wringtail

Horses wring their tails to show that they are agitated. Nobody likes to ride a horse that's forever wringing his tail. Horses with very short tails are also apt to wring them.

A colt is ready to be broken to ride. The owner trains the colt in fine fashion and the way the colt goes pleases him. Immediately, he wants to improve the colt's appearance. He pulls the colt's tail very short. The colt feels the difference in weight and length of his tail and wants to switch it. About this time, training gets harder — more drill and arena work. The colt gets a little sore and wrings his tail. The owner spurs him for doing so. This irritates the colt **44** more than ever and he becomes a "wringtail."

When I pull a tail, I do so gradually and I never go to extremes (anymore). A hock-length tail is short enough for me. If a colt seems a little grumpy, I leave his tail alone. I seldom use spurs on a young colt.

When I try to correct a "wringtail," I let the tail grow, make sure the saddle fits right, that the blankets and cinch are clean and that there's nothing about the bridle or hackamore that rubs or causes him discomfort. I give the colt lots of trail riding and mighty little drill for quite some time. The colt should enjoy the ride. If he does, he'll gradually stop wringing his tail.

The "Doggy" Horse

When I call a horse a "doggy" horse, I mean one that plods along, hating every minute of the ride. When pushed forward, the horse shows displeasure, laying his ears back, kicking up, balking or sulking.

Sometimes a horse is bred to be this way. Some stallions seem to produce such offspring. They don't like their work and show it at every opportunity. Only a strong rider can get work out of them.

I once broke a nice filly for a dude ranch. The owner noticed and liked her. He took her over and rode her twenty miles up and down a mountain. The filly wasn't ready for this and that one ride turned her into a "doggy" horse. Too much riding can turn a good horse into one that hates to be ridden.

Handling a colt in a very rough fashion can turn a good prospect into a sullen zombie. I once started a half-Arabian filly for a lady. The filly was playfull, mischievious, but not in the least mean or hard to handle.

I'd ridden the filly for a week when the lady decided to try her. I wasn't around when she tried this. She saddled the filly with an English saddle and rigged her with a full bridle. I'd been using a stock saddle and hackamore. The filly walked about twenty feet and bucked the lady down. The lady was hurt and had to be hospitalized. This made the lady think that I couldn't train horses so she sent the filly out to board at a "horseman-farmer's" place. The farmer's son tried to ride the filly and she put him down. The farmer beat the filly half to death and turned her into a spiritless nag. She was sold to a "hack" stable.

There are many reasons why some horses are sullen. Some are bred this way. Some are made this way by man. A man-made horse of this type should be turned out for quite some time to give the animal time to forget. Then some easy trail rides would be the next step. There is some chance that the horse might recover his original good disposition. ■

CHAPTER SIX

CORRECTING PERFORMANCE FAULTS

Out Of Position Horses

One might say, as a general rule, that a horse should follow his head. This sounds easy but think of all the horses that you've ridden. Don't most of them, when neck-reined, hold their heads in the opposite direction to that in which they're travelling? Rein to the left and the horse's head will be pulled to the right. This is the inevitable result of the indirect (neck-rein) rein.

As time goes on, the horse gets worse. Eventually, the good colt looks like the horses we see on TV or at the movies. This is caused by laziness, poor rein handling and the neck-rein. The situation can be remedied by a combination of not being lazy, good rein handling and by use of the direct rather than the indirect rein.

The English Pelham and the Weymouth bits are the answer and there are many varieties to choose from. In fact, there are some western bits made to accommodate double reins. There is a slot for a rein in the vicinity of the mouthpiece. The horse is pulled into position with the top rein. The bottom rein is used to bring the chin in and for positive curb control.

There are soft and hard rubber-mouthed Pelhams available. The full double bridle, with both curb and snaffle bits (Weymouth), is a fine rig for correcting a horse.

You might think that it looks a bit odd to see a horse ridden in a stock saddle and English bridle. We don't care about appearances. We do care how the horse works and will put anything on his head that will do the job.

People hold double reins in different fashions. Most people cross their reins. The rein to the leverage part of the bit (lower) is held between first and second or second and third fingers while the rein to the non-leverage part of the bit (ring or slot at the mouthpiece) runs from the bottom of the hand. I like the leverage part of the bit very low so I hold them without crossing them.

We use the Pelham to correct a spoiled horse, or train a colt, so we're not interested in neck-reining. Two reins are held in each hand.

They are snug but not tight. When the horse is cantered to the right,

This horse is circling in the arena. Notice that he's bent in the direction he's travelling. He's "following his head."

his head will often be canted to the left so we must pull the head into his way of going so that he will "follow his head." We use light pulls and releases to accomplish this, and the non-leverage (top) part of the bit is used. Actually, the leverage (bottom) part of the bit is used very little, mainly for bringing his chin in, slowing down and stopping. *All pulling* is done with the top part of the bit. If the horse's head is carried too high, a running martingale can be used on the top rein.

Concerning leg aids, we think about the left leg to push the horse to the right. If the rider wants to circle to the left, he will push with the right leg to signal the horse his intentions. But, this is how it *should* be. Actually, the horse that we're trying to get to follow his head will generally swing over, trying to keep his head from the direction he's travelling. The leg will "force" the horse into a tight circle. He'll side-slip over and our large circle will immediately be cut down to a very small one.

We must achieve results. The horse can be started into the correct lead by using the correct leg aid; left leg for right circle. But, when the horse starts to slip away in, he must be *held out* with the other leg. We end up using left leg for the left circle. When I tell people about this, I say to "bend the horse around your leg."

When such leg pressure is used, the rider must use a *stronger* aid to signify that the horse should travel left. This aid is body weight, or the act of leaning to the left. The horse is put into the left lead with the right leg, held out with the left leg and cued by body weight. All the while, the rider leans forward, hands low, keeping a light contact, pulling the horse's head slightly into the circle with light pulls on the top rein and forces the horse up into the bit by squeezing with his legs, using body momentum to push the horse ahead. The horse must be driven up into the bridle and kept there while he's working.

Some horses just don't respond well enough to leg pressure and forcefully pushing the horse ahead with body "English." Additional aids of whip and spur may be needed. These tools are aids and should be used as such.

Some improvement is noticed at each session. A lot of time is needed to correct the horse that works out of position. Repetition will eventually replace bad habits with good habits.

Behind The Bit

An old California trainer once told me, "A horse that ain't up in the bit can't do anything." By this, he meant that a reining horse can't work on a loose rein and do any kind of passable work.

We admire people who ride cutting horses and copy their mode of rein handling. The cutting horse is shown on a very loose rein because it must be apparent to the judges that the horse is working on his own — not being reined. But the reining horse is not a cutting horse. Light contact (when being worked) must be maintained at all times. Signals come too jerkily and too late when they're applied from a loose rein.

It used to be fashionable to show pleasure horses on a very loose rein. Trainers would canter their pupils for hours on a loose rein. Soon, the horse became accustomed to this method of working and that's all he would do. Ask him to stop, turn, and the head would go up. He'd flop around rather than rein correctly. When the reins would be pulled up for some reason, it always came as a surprise to the horse.

Such a horse is difficult to train. He's behind the bit. The trainer must *leg* him up into the bridle so that the horse is *being held back just a little bit*. He is then collected, or as someone once said, "he's imprisoned between legs and hands." This is how the bridle horse should work.

48   Hand position should be low — right down at the horse's withers.

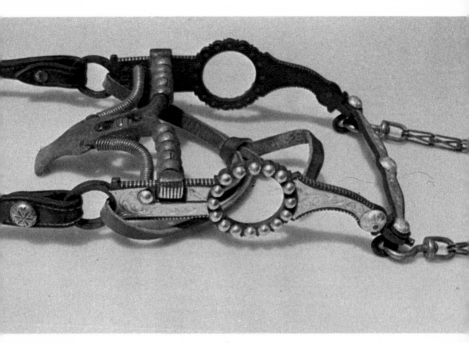

The Dave Jones spade bit has more copper than the average. There are copper rollers and crickets in addition to the usual copper braces. A raised portion gives tongue relief.

The hands should give and take with the horse's head.

Probably the finest bit ever devised for the true reinsman is the spade as it is used on the West Coast. The bit is always handmade by master craftsmen. The high spade mouthpiece insures that the young horse can't get his tongue over the bit. The copper braces afford a pleasing taste to the horse and affect his salivary glands so that he constantly makes mouth-moisture. There is a Colombian saying that a horse that doesn't make mouth moisture is no good.

The large cricket is the mouthpiece making a clicking chirping noise that horses like. It's called a "pacifier." The nervous horse works this cricket, makes his noises and calms down.

The spade bit is balanced so that a horse is a little uncomfortable when his head isn't carried in the right position. He learns to carry the bit gradually, no reins being used, while ridden in a light bosal. After a month or so, reins are attached and used sparingly. Months later, the horse becomes "straight up in the bridle." **49**

There are take-offs on the spade. One is the "half-breed." I have never used such a bit as I see no real need for it. The "Salinas" is a mouthpiece with a high copper-covered port which covers a cricket. Almost all horses like the Salinas and will readily accept it and work in it. However, the one thing the Salinas doesn't have is the balance to make a horse want to carry his head in that "Just right" position.

A lady wrote to a question-and-answer column in a horse magazine. Her question was something like this:

"My horse works well in both the spade and Salinas bits. However, when I ride him in the Salinas, he has a tendency to overflex — to bring his chin in too much. Why?"

The answer given to the lady doesn't jibe with my experience. My answer would have been that the Salinas is comfortable no matter how the horse holds his head. The Salinas is a fine bit but many horses will eventually overflex when it's used.

The colt bit, commonly called the snaffle, should be used like the hackamore, which is never used with a steady pull on the reins. The action is always "pull and release."

Horse Turns On The Wrong End

I'm working a horse now that turns on the wrong end. This horse never had any formal training until now. He's gentle, willing, stops pretty good, backs readily, but he works on the wrong end! When I stop and turn him, he plants those front hooves and slops around with his rear. The habit is so deeply entrenched that conventional means of handling this problem just doesn't work. He simply doesn't know that he *can* work off the hind legs.

The main reason a horse turns on the forehand is that he has been turned too sharply without stopping and rolling back. His rider has ridden him down a fence and made a 180 degree turn without stopping. Since the particular horse I'm talking about doesn't respond to aids, stern measures must be used.

I ride the horse down the fence and stop him some five feet parallel to it. After waiting a bit, I whack him a good one on the shoulders with a training whip. This scares him enough to force him to turn on the rear end. This action must be repeated over and over. The horse soon dreads to stop along the fence and there's a battle about that. Naturally, training this horse to work correctly will take some time. To date, I've had a chap snap and a spur ripped off by the chain link fence because the horse would swing his whole body into it when making one of his bad turns. He improves a little each day, and that's all we can hope for. He must learn to use himself correctly. When turning off the hindquarters is thoroughly learned, this horse will be on his way toward making a reining horse.

The conventional way I generally use doesn't work with this horse for he'll hit a fence — run into the fence with me. A colt I start will never do this. Here's how I teach the turn on the haunches to a young horse.

The colt is ridden parallel to the fence and stopped about five feet from it. I hold him there a bit. Then I jump him into the fence to force him to do a 180 degree turn. He must run out of it. I'll let him lope around the arena a few times before pulling him down. Then I'll stop and turn him the other way. The colt always stops and stands before being jumped out in the opposite direction. The speed he uses when he wheels to jump out forces him to pivot on his hindquarters. When he does this fast enough, he'll make a 180 degree turn before his front hooves come down.

After a few weeks of this, the colt automatically turns on his hind legs. The period of time between the stop and turn is called the "dwell." The dwell can last five minutes or it can be a fraction of a second. When it is a fraction of a second, the colt is doing the "set and turn." The colt lopes down the fence and the rider signals the stop. The colt is turned into the fence as soon as his front hooves hit the ground. This is enough time for him to gather himself and use those front hooves to throw himself the other way. This is a very catty maneuver. Some horses are magnificent at it while others can never do it well. The horse that *really* slides well is seldom a good "set and turn" horse.

When the colt has mastered the 180 degree turn, he can be taught to pivot on his hindquarters for a full circle. This is the start of the spin.

The colt is ridden down the fence, stopped, turned into the fence, jumped out, held when his hooves hit the ground and jumped out away from the fence. Speed is essential. The horse *must* be jumped out at the completion of the circle. Speed is what keeps him turning properly. He's not going to do this perfectly the first time. Much work and review of the half-circle with jump-out is necessary.

When the colt can perform the full-circle, a circle-and-a-half can be attempted. The colt, of course, must jump out with speed after each maneuver. Forget the speed in the jump-out and the crispness of the turns will soon diminish and the colt will flop around his circles. Work correctly and you will work up to the spin, with as many revolutions as necessary. All this seems a long way off for the colt I'm riding, but he'll make it someday.

Perhaps many of you are faced with the same problem I'm working

If you have a colt that just won't turn off the hind end, equip yourself with a crop and push it into his shoulder to get him to move that front end.

on; that of a colt that just *won't* turn off the hind end. Different methods are called for.

Equip yourself with a riding crop, or at least a stick. While on the ground, press the heavy end of the crop into his shoulder and push. He'll move away from the pressure. He may move his whole body but he'll also move that front end. Practice this on both sides until the horse moves away from the crop at the slightest pressure. Then try to move with him to keep his front end moving and his back legs in one place. Before long, you can actually move the colt around, turning him on his haunches. Alas, we must still teach him to do this from the saddle.

Use the crop when you ride. Move the colt around by pressing the end of the crop into his shoulder. A helper on the ground may really be of help. Reward the colt when he works correctly. Soon, a light **52** tap with the crop should make him turn on the haunches. When

This horse shows he can "spike 'em in" while doing a set for the set and turn. Many horses won't stop correctly because they've been stopped too much without boots to protect the fetlocks. The horse gets sore and bounces to protect himself.

he knows how to handle himself, the method of using the fence with the jump-out can be employed to bring correct work into the picture.

An excellent drill for the colt that has learned how to work is to circle him, starting with a large circle and working down to a small circle, stop and spin. When the colt has learned to work correctly, the drill will do a great deal to keep him sharp.

Bad Stop

Getting a good stop is hard enough. Keeping it is even harder. People want to know why their horses won't slide. Others want to know why the horse *did* slide in training but won't after they get home.

The reason most horses won't stop correctly is that their owners try to slide them too much. Often, the owner will run his horse and set him up time after time, generally without boots to protect the horse's fetlocks. The horse gets sore and bounces to protect himself. He sees no reason to come to a hard stop time after time. **53**

A colt is ridden parallel to the fence and stopped about five feet from it. He is then jumped into the fence to force him to do a 180 degree turn. He must run out of it!

When a horse has a reason to stop, he will, if he's any kind of an athlete. The cutting horse must make hard stops from hard runs time after time when blocking a running cow. The rope-horse stops hard every time he makes a run. He, too, has a reason to stop. The reined cowhorse stops in fine fashion when working a cow. Since he does work so many cattle, this work carries over into his dry work and allows him to keep working correctly much longer than the reining horse that gets no cow work.

The primary things a person should work toward are suppleness, lightness and responsiveness. This means a lot of reining work. If a colt only knows how to go "down the road," he won't be responsive.

The colt watches his rider's hand. The hand working the rein is low and out near the colt's head. The colt learns to turn toward the hand for the rider takes the colt's head with pulls and releases. The colt gives his head when the rider pulls it. The rider uses his legs to keep the colt loping. Soon, a grip with the legs becomes a signal for the colt to alert himself.

The rider moves the colt down the arena. He signals the colt with a light pull on the hackamore rein. Then he grips the colt with his legs and pulls harder. If the colt doesn't stop, the rider will jerk him around in his tracks with a LOW strong pull. This is called the *double*. After the colt has been doubled a few times, he'll dread it. He'll learn to stop when the rider grips him with his legs and pulls straight back on the one rein. The rider pulls back on one rein then slacks off. If the colt's nose goes up, the other rein is pulled to bring the nose down. This could be compared to "sawing" on the reins.

In a few days, the colt will start to shoot his hind legs up under himself and will stop in wonderful fashion from a walk. Such practice should only be attempted a few times each ride. When the colt works correctly, leave him alone.

Then the rider should work from a slow trot. He'll do exactly the same things he did at a walk. When the horse stops correctly at a trot, he can be worked at a canter. He'll soon do a nice stop from the slow canter.

One might think that the next logical step is to run the colt and slide him. *Not so!* Speed would come down on him. He'd want to run and you'd ruin all the good work you'd done. The colt must learn to "set and turn," a maneuver previously described. When the colt is a good "set and turn" horse, more speed can be worked for. Wide open running is never desirable in practice. I never run a colt unless I'm working cattle. Lope, yes. Run, no.

As the colt learns suppleness, his rider should remember *to do* **55** *something* after every stop. Don't just stop and then ride forward. Stop and turn, stop and spin or stop and back up. Never let the colt think that he can stop and then go forward or he'll soon lose his stop. If a colt knows that he must turn immediately after stopping, he'll prepare himself for it rather than bouncing along to a jolting stop.

Monte Foreman, through his fine action photography, has shown that a horse, with rider aboard, must make three distinct efforts to get stopped from a hard run. This is on average, not prepared ground. The horse must slide, take some steps for balance, slide, more steps and slide to a stop. The rider should handle his reins accordingly. He should pull, release, pull, release, pull and release. By doing so, he's helping and not hindering his horse.

The roping horse will generally stop harder. He stops not only himself but the calf as well, so he'll get down onto the ground quicker to brace himself for the shock. He can handle himself better than the horse carrying a rider for he's not hampered by the rider's weight throwing him off balance. When the rope-horse stops, the rider either has his weight in the stirrup or he's clear off the horse.

Re-training a horse with a poor stop is much like training the colt. He must look for signals from his rider. Teaching the "set and turn" is a fine way to train for the stop. If your horse knows the "set and turn," the rider simply holds him straight, rather than turning after the stop.

When a horse can do a good "set and turn" on the fence, he should learn how to do the same work in the center of the arena. When he can do this, he'll know how to do roll-backs as they are required in a reining pattern. ■

CHAPTER SEVEN

ON NOT SPOILING HORSES

Horses are easy to spoil. Sensible riding practices should be employed. The following eight points are those which I consider very important. They derive from many years of experience and, if followed, can prevent the development of many problems.

1. NEVER run your horse to the barn. I know of no way to spoil a horse quicker. If you must run on a trail ride, do so while heading away from the barn.

2. Use proper equipment. The saddle should fit the horse. Blankets and cinches should be clean. The bridle and bit shouldn't pinch the horse.

3. Never tie your horse up by the reins. Carry a halter for this purpose. The light bosal with fiador can be used to tie up a horse. The movie and TV people do us a great disservice by showing their heroes tying horses at the saloon by the bridle reins. If something startles the horse, he can jump back and ruin his mouth forever.

4. Many people ground-tie their horses. after a bit of teaching, the horse learns to stand when the reins are dropped. BUT IMAGINE what happens when a horse steps on the reins. He can break the sensitive bars in his mouth. I favor hobbles and stay completely away from ground-tying.

5. Games on horseback are a lot of fun but you can ruin a good horse playing these games. How? The horse RUNS OUT OF THE ARENA or, toward the gate out of the arena. Few horses can "keep their cool" under such circumstances and, at best, become prancing, hard-to-hold screwballs. Sure, we all know of horses that retain their good sense and still run at the games. These are the exceptions rather than the rule. Let me cite one example.

A well-known barrel racer had run first in a short arena. The judges noted how her horse had to slow up to get stopped at the arena gate. They decided to leave the gate open during the rest of the runs. The first racer rode in to protest just as one girl was finishing her run. The racing horse, uncontrollable, slammed into the first girl's horse, injuring it badly and killing the running horse. Needless to say, both girls were badly injured. When you get on a horse

We see movie horses rear. This is "pretty" to some people, but it is dangerous. If your horse starts rearing, cure him quickly or have a professional take it out of him.

that you don't have control of at all times, you are a menace to yourself and others.

6. We see movie horses rear. This is "pretty" so some people encourage it. They will hold the horse back and spur it ahead. When it rears, they reward the horse. The horse soon believes that it should rear. Soon, the rears become higher and someday, the horse loses balance and falls over backwards on the rider. Leave such stuff for the movie riders. If your horse starts rearing, cure him quickly or have a professional take it out of him.

7. Kids who have horses also have friends. These friends like to ride, too. But letting people who know *nothing* about riding ride your horse is just asking for trouble. Of course they'll spoil your horse. That fact is so simple it needs no explaining. Persuade your friends to take riding lessons from experienced teachers. They'll learn how to ride correctly and will thank you for it later.

8. Many people get too "fresh" with horses. Some kids have nice gentle horses that they can do anything with. You'll see youngsters with such horses riding double, triple, laying all over the horse, sliding down the rump, jumping on from the rear, riding backwards and other such foolishness. Sometimes these young people think that any horse can be treated in such a manner. They'll ride a young colt double and get bucked off. Since "ole Paint" can be ridden anywhere with a halter, they think a young brave stallion should handle just like "Paint." He won't! Someone gets hurt. Fooling around with strange horses isn't wise. Always completely know the horse before getting "fresh" with him, and even then some of these old pets can surprise you.

I'm very cautious because the law of averages is running against me. Put a novice on a bad horse. He'll get bucked off, but chances are he won't get hurt. If this novice keeps riding horses, chances are that he WILL get hurt because nobody can break horses for thirty years without being injured. That's the law of averages working.

A school chum of mine (30 years ago) wanted to ride a bad horse I'd just purchased. I told him that the horse was too mean for him. He then asked if he could sit on him if I held him. I allowed that this would be O.K. He started to walk in back of the horse. I warned him that the horse would kick. So, he *crawled under him* to get to the near side. He actually tried to crawl under that bronc!

The horse jumped and started bucking backwards. The kid was caught between the front and back legs and rolled like a hoop for about fifty feet. Then he was kicked way out, landing on the cement driveway. He moaned and groaned a little, but his only real injury was a blood blister on the end of his finger where a tiny bit of skin happened to be between the horse's hoof and the driveway. I'd have been killed for doing anything so foolish. ∎

CHAPTER EIGHT

UNDERSTANDING HORSES

The trainer, after years of association with horses, begins to think like a horse. He knows horses do certain things. Scientists consider the horse a stupid animal. A horse is not stupid, but he is a little "funny" at times.

A horse might be separated from his horse-friend by a fence with an open gate. He'll panic to get to his chum and may try to jump the fence. He'll get caught in the fence, kick and fight, tearing himself up, get loose, run to his friend and try to kick him out of the pasture. All of this happens with a gate standing open only a few yards away. This is a pretty stupid way to act.

We learn from this that a horse can get panicky when separated from a horse he knows, even if he has a daily fight with the other horse. Your gentle horse can become uncontrollable when he's separated from a horse he's been running with. To overcome this problem, your horse should be stabled for a few days before attempting to handle him after a traumatic separation.

We also learn that the straight line between two objects is the course the horse will take. If he wants to go to another horse, he'll go STRAIGHT to the horse. This is especially true if the horse is panicky. One should stay back away from the horse to give him time to calm down.

Most horses, if caught in wire, will fight until they're exhausted and ruined. Hobble training is very valuable, for a horse well trained to be restrained by hobbles will be far less prone to injury himself if caught in wire.

Horses like to fight with other horses. When loose in a pasture, there's little to do about it. They'll fight over feed so plenty of feed boxes are a must.

If the trainer genuinely likes horses, he'll find that his horses like him. The man who is soured with his profession makes a poor trainer. Horses know when a person is in a good or a bad mood. When a human is afraid or angry, the horse will be terrified.

It takes time to accustom horses to things. A colt may act wild when first handled by a person. But doing so daily calms him down.

Horses like to fight with other horses. They'll fight over feed, so plenty of feed boxes are a must. If fighting becomes extreme, separate them.

The bronc may explode when his trainer first tries to sack him out, but time and patience will prevail. In a few days, the bronc knows that a flapping feed sack won't hurt him.

Repetition is the thing with horses. Teach him new things with caution. Don't give him too much to think about. But training shouldn't *bog down* with the same old things over and over. The colt would never get out of the breaking pen if the trainer fears to try new things.

Some horses will bully people if they find that they can get away with such actions. If a little colt runs at a person, and the person runs from him, the colt will rationalize that he's very tough and that people are afraid of him. He'll soon delight in chasing people. Such stuff is only a close step away from rearing and striking, trying to hit a person with his hooves.

If a horse trys to chase you, even swinging your jacket should **61**

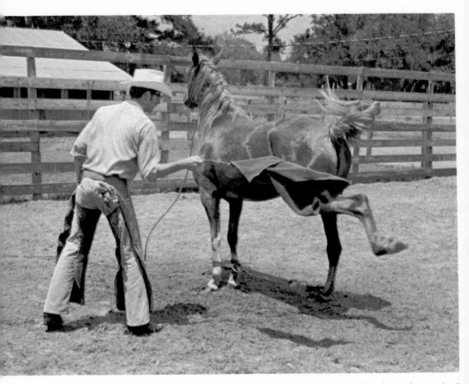

It takes time to accustom horses to things, and a great deal of patience is required. This filly kicks with her one free foot while being sacked-out because she wouldn't let anyone touch her legs.

scare him away. A long training whip will immediately teach him that he can't chase a person and get away with it.

Horses that are bad about wheeling and kicking should be whip-broken. The rear of the horse is whipped until the horse faces the person. This need not be done in a cruel fashion. The horse is treated kindly, petted or rewarded with a bite of something good when he faces his trainer. The horse learns that good things happen to him when he comes to the person; bad things when he wheels away and kicks.

We'll see a horse do things that will amaze us with his brilliance. The same horse can be so stupid about other things that we're amazed with his stupidity. We who train horses are used to these contradictions. ■

CHAPTER NINE

CONFORMATION PROBLEMS

The trainer will often have a horse given him to work that *can't* do certain things because of conformation defects. Most trainers will tell the owner that there are certain things his horse can't be because of his build.

1. A horse with a shallow girth will lack the stamina to run long distances or do anything in endurance events. The horse should have ample heart and lung room. A horse with a shallow girth will generally have a weak back because he doesn't have enough structural depth to carry a man for long distances.

2. The previously discussed ewe-necked horse has difficulty as a reining horse because it's a natural thing for his head to come up. Making a reining horse of such an animal can be done but at the cost of double work, time and expense. It's really fighting nature.

3. There are many things that can be wrong with the front legs. The horse can toe in or toe out. The horse can have buck knees, calf knees, bench knees, or can be tied-in-at-the-knees. A horse that's bad in front is a dangerous horse for he's prone to fall. Calf knees are the worst defects because the horse's weight is working *against* the joints.

4. If a horse isn't just right behind, he'll be subject to serious lameness. The horse that has crooked hind legs is subject to curby hocks, thoroughpin and spavin. The horse that has hind legs that are too straight is subject to thoroughpin, spavin and the breaking down of the pastern. The horse with the too-straight hind legs is more of a problem than the horse that's a little crooked.

5. Some horses cut up toward the flank like a Greyhound dog. This is all right for the race horse but the working horse should be deep through the flank. He's much more able to work if he has a powerful rear end.

Looking at the horse from the rear, his depth through the stifle should be more than it is through the point of the hips. The carrot-rumped horse isn't powerful behind.

The gaskin should have almost as much inside as outside muscle. Cannon bone should be short for a long cannon spells trouble. Pasterns should be neither too long, nor too short. The short pastern

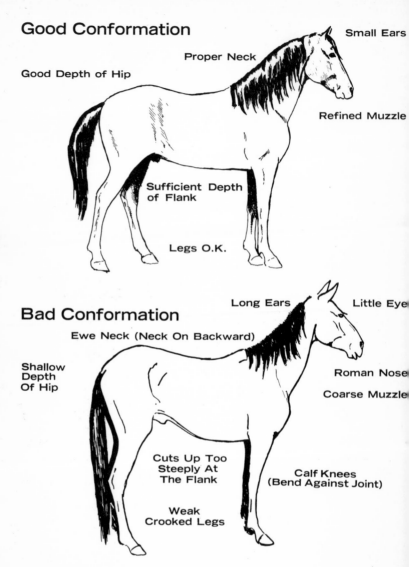

Good Conformation

Small Ears

Proper Neck

Good Depth of Hip

Refined Muzzle

Sufficient Depth of Flank

Legs O.K.

Long Ears   **Little Eye**

Bad Conformation

Ewe Neck (Neck On Backward)

Shallow Depth Of Hip

Roman Nose

Coarse Muzzle

Cuts Up Too Steeply At The Flank

Calf Knees (Bend Against Joint)

Weak Crooked Legs

means a rough ride (the pastern can be compared to a shock absorber) while a long pastern is prone to break down.

The horse with perfect conformation is impossible to find. We will do well to come up with as close to perfect conformation as we can find. It's just that much easier to work with. ∎